SUMMARY

Hidden Figures

The American Dream and the Untold Story of the Black Women Mathematicians Who Helped Win the Space Race

Book by

Margot Lee Shetterly

The Summary Guy

TABLE OF CONTENTS

INTRODUCTION

This book is an autobiography about African-American women who greatly contributed to the US winning the space race. Back in the 1940s, women began joining the workforce because there was great lack of workers due to the many men who were fighting in the Second World War. There was one place that was in desperate need of intelligent and hard-working people. That place was NACA. Many African-American women applied for the jobs there with different levels of success. Some women succeeded in laying down entry-level jobs in engineering positions, while several of them ended up contributing to the American launch that sent the first man to the moon.

As we read the book, we can see that the author organized every chapter in a somewhat loose chronological order, and that every chapter is based around a central theme. The book could be a problem if the reader does not possess adequate knowledge about rocket science. But those who continue reading will find that this is an inspiring story.

SUMMARY

PART 1: THE CHRONICLES

The book opens with the author of the book, Margot Lee Shetterly, and her husband visiting her parents in Hampton, Virginia. While they were driving, her father reminded her of the women in their hometown who worked as computers for NASA. Margot's father was a scientist at NASA back in 1960s. This meant that Margot was familiar with many African-American people who worked there as well. As a matter of fact, Shetterly recalled that while growing up, the face of science was also brown, like hers.

As the conversation with her father continues, the both of them remembered many past events. Since the author had a personal and cultural connection with the African American women who were working for NASA in 1940s, 1950s, and 1960s, she decided to chronicle their stories.

The story jumps into the past. It is year 1943. One unnamed personnel officer at Langley Memorial Aeronautical Laboratory was ordered to find and hire new employees. He was ordered to do so because President Roosevelt wanted a huge increase in plane production. But because many men were fighting in WWII, the company could not hire enough men, simply because there were not enough educated men to do the job. The company had to make a decision about what to do next and how to decrease personnel shortage. The company decided to hire women, African American women included. After this, many qualified African American women decided to apply for the job. They needed a job because they needed financial and social security and prestige for their families.

Shetterly then introduces a woman named Dorothy Vaughn. She was a college-educated African American woman and a math teacher. Vaughn was working in an Army laundry room for the summer. She was described as beautiful and independent African American woman, as well as a mother of four children. As a person, Vaughn was very confident and intelligent. Though she had a chance to attend graduate school, she refused because she wanted to help her family financially. After she saw an advertisement for a job at Langley, she immediately applied.

PART 2: LIVING IN NEW TOWN AND LEADING NEW LIFE

Even though Vaughn was highly respected educator who was strongly attached to her adopted town of Farmville, she decided to accept the job as mathematician under wartime contract. Moving to Newport News in Virginia was something that she needed to accept. Vaughn struggled a bit because she did not want to leave her children, but she knew that they were surrounded by many caregivers. Another problem for her was leaving her husband. Their marriage was already strained due to his constant travels for his job. The two also had very different interests. But despite all of that, Vaughn decided that this was her chance, and so she moved to Newport News.

After she arrived in Newport News, Vaughn realized that the city was dedicated to the business of war. The city was overcrowded and overpopulated, leading to tension among the people, especially racial tension. Another problem was that there was an overload of work, and since there was a war going on, food was scarce.

Dorothy was assigned to the West Area of Langley because it was where the African American women worked. Here we find out that approximately one month before Vaughn arrived to Newport News, the Secretary of the Navy, Frank Knox, had visited Langley. All workers, regardless of age, race, and gender, had gathered together to listen to his speech. The irony was that after he gave his speech, the African American women who had gone to the cafeteria and sat at their usual table were labeled as "Colored Computers." The women did what they could to ignore the sign and its broader implications. But one day, a woman named Miriam Mann decided that she had had enough. She started stealing the sign and putting it in her purse. After a while, the sign did not return and the women were able to eat their lunch like everyone else – with dignity.

PART 3: THE TUSKEGEE AIRMEN AND WWII ENDING

The chapter opens with a description of the Tuskegee airmen, who took the African American community by storm. The men brought the community pride and hope for equality.

Workers from Langley infiltrated the town of Hampton. Locals were left confused with their perceived strangeness. Vaughn and several other workers soon began their courses in engineering physics. They learned about aerodynamics and wind tunnels, and Vaughn found herself immersed in her studies.

Traveling from Newport News and her hometown proved to be very exhausting for Vaughn. She finally decided to move to Newport News permanently, bringing her children with her. They decided to settle in an apartment in an African American area called Newsome Park. Although her husband, Howard, visited them every now and then, their lives remained separate in many ways.

The joy of the Second World War ending was marred by the layoffs of two million African American women. Many African American women were afraid that they would lose the respect they had earned in the workplace. Because of this, Vaughn hoped that her wartime contract would be made permanent.

PART 4: THOSE WHO DECIDE TO MOVE FORWARD

This chapter opens with a description of a woman named Katherine Goble. She spent four years at home with her children before finally returning to classroom to take over her husband's contract.

When Goble was growing up, she showed the same love for science and math that her father possessed. Her father moved the family so that the children could continue to be educated. Goble attended West Virginia State College, and there, she was mentored by Dr. William Claytor, who prepared her for a career as a research mathematician. After graduating, Goble worked as a teacher before she was chosen to be one of three African American students to be integrated at West Virginia University. Goble began her graduate program, but needed to postpone it because she found out that she and her husband were expecting a baby.

After this, the story again goes back to Vaughn. Even though she and Howard do not see each other very often, they had two more children. After she spends time with each child, she returned to work. Vaughn's family greatly depended on her income, and she had a large network of caregivers for her children. Even though she was making a lot of money, she was still very careful and conscious about how easily that money could be taken away. Vaughn wore old clothing and ate her children's leftovers because she wanted to make sure that her children had everything they needed.

Vaughn was made a permanent employee in 1946. There were many women around the country who were working in the field of aerodynamics, but it was much more difficult for them to advance in their careers than it was for men. But despite this, many women succeeded in having prosperous and successful careers at Langley. After Vaughn's immediate supervisor had died, she was appointed as the acting head of West Computing, leading her to eventually become the head of West Computing.

PART 5: MARY WINSTON JACKSON

The next chapter opens with a description of a woman named Mary Winston Jackson. Jackson grew up in Hampton and attended the Hampton Institute. There, she double-majored the mathematics and physical science. Like many of her family members, Jackson also became a math teacher.

She worked for one year in Maryland, but eventually moved back to Hampton to take care of her sick father. Since Jackson was unable to get a job in her hometown, and thanks to the fact that her family members worked for the school system, she became the secretary and bookkeeper for the King Street USO. Jackson excelled at her job. She also frequently performed many other duties outside of her assigned position. After she started a family, she became the leader of a Girl Scout troop. She did everything in her power to make sure that the girls in her troop were exposed to different and more normal ways of life.

In 1951, Jackson began working as a clerk typist at Fort Monroe. This job required her to have a security clearance. By that time, the Soviet Union and the US started their aeronautical competition, which was a good thing, in a way, because it opened many new jobs at Langley. Jackson took the job working for Dorothy Vaughn as a NACA computer. NACA's primary goal was to make supersonic flight something that will be real and possible.

At the same time, the tension surrounding the Rosenberg trial put the country on edge. America's racial problems became the main cause of international embarrassment. Because of that, President Truman issued Executive Order 9980. This Order held federal department heads responsible for ending workplace discrimination.

PART 6: MARY AND DOROTHY

In next chapter of the book, we read that on one occasion, Vaughn sent Jackson to the East Side, along with several other white co-workers. When Mary asked for directions to the bathroom, the white people laughed. They did not know whether Jackson should use the bathroom because bathrooms were segregated. This event left Jackson very upset. She was angry for the rest of the day, even when she saw Kazimierz "Kaz" Czarnecki. After seeing Kaz, Jackson immediately went to see him. Kaz offered her a job, and she gladly accepted it.

Langley laboratory did a great job when it came to aerodynamics and wind tunnels. Dorothy Hoover, who was an African American theoretical engineer at Langley, wrote two notable reports with male scientists about swept-back wings. After some time, Hoover resigned from engineering and decided to attend graduate school and earn a Master's degree in mathematics. At the same time, Jackson thrived at her job as engineer. She was given an assignment by one of her superiors, John Becker. When she finished her assignment, Becker challenged her calculations. Mary insisted that her calculations were correct and it soon turned out to be Becker's fault. Mary was also known for having the ability to stand up for herself, and this later marked her as someone worthy of a promotion.

PART 7: TEACHER KATHERINE GOBLE

This chapter begins with a description of a family wedding. During the wedding, teacher Katherine Goble was offered a job at Langley. She also began working under the supervision of Dorothy Vaughn, but was quickly reassigned to the Flight Research Division.

On her first day on the job, Goble sat next to a white male engineer, but he moved away from her. Goble was not sure if he moved away because she was a woman, an African American, or because she was a lower position than him. Regardless, she decided to be prudent and not pursue the issue. Within just two weeks, the two of them began socializing and soon became friends.

Vaughn managed to negotiate a promotion and a raise for Goble, and she was given a permanent position at the Flight Research Division. Her mathematic abilities, together with her strong desire to learn, helped her fit in well in a department that was mostly made up of men.

Goble refused to use the segregated bathroom. She also did not eat in lunch room in order to avoid any potential racial conflict. When her husband, Jimmy, died as a result of brain tumor, she was devastated. But regardless of her husband's death, Katherine insisted that her daughters continue to work hard and succeed in their academics so that they can also have good future.

After this, we read that Langley started using electronic computers. Even though the human computers still had their jobs, Vaughn sensed that learning to use the electronic computers was mandatory for job security. So, she decided to enroll in computing courses.

In Vaughn's hometown of Farmville, the African American students were riding in very old school buses, which were extremely dangerous. One of these buses crashed and killed Barbara John's best friend. John gathered other students from her high school to protest for the same safety and education that the white students had at their high schools. The protest was noticed by two Virginia lawyers who worked with Thurgood Marshall. He then compiled John's protests together with several similar cases across the country. He wanted to form the U.S. Supreme Court case *Brown vs. the Board of Education*, which would lead to the integration of all schools in the United States. The state of Virginia resisted following the order to investigate.

Kaz Czarencki put Mary Jackson to work in the wind tunnels before asking Jackson to begin training her to be an engineer. But because of the segregation policy in Virginia, Mary had to receive dispensation to attend engineering training at school, where there were only white men and women.

PART 8: THE END OF SEGREGATION AT LANGLEY

The story then jumps to another African American woman, Christine Mann. She attended boarding school in North Carolina, and as she was arranging the library's newspapers and magazines, she read an article about Sputnik. Many African American newspapers were blaming the missile gap on school segregation. Since the Soviet Union did not segregate schools, the newspapers reported that this was the main reason why the Soviet Union had the upper hand. They had easy access to every brilliant mind in their country, and not just brilliant white minds. As she read the article, Mann felt that she wanted to be involved in the space race with the Soviet Union. She enjoyed an upbringing filled with learning, and after she graduated, Mann decided to attend Hampton Institute.

The story jumps to 1957, as the US was still having problems when it came to space race with the Soviets. Langley began shifting its focus from aeronautics to space travel. The African American employees slowly became more and more accepted and appreciated by their fellow white employees. This happened thanks to the civil rights movement, which greatly changed NACA. Since NACA focused more on aeronautics and the main goal was now to focus on space travel, the name was changed into NASA. On May 5th, 1958, the West Area Computers Unit was disbanded, which was a sign of end of segregation at Langley.

PART 9: ANOTHER OBSTACLE HAD BEEN OVERCOME

The story returns to Goble and her colleagues, who began researching space travel. Goble asked to attend editorial meetings with her male coworkers and was told that she could not do that because she was a woman. But thanks to her intelligence and persistence, she was eventually allowed to attend the meetings.

After this, the story focuses on 1958 and NASA's Space Task Group. The group began working on Project Mercury with their main goal being sending a man into space. In the same year, Virginia closed the public schools that had integrated. This left thousands of students without education. In the meantime, Goble met army captain Jim Johnson at church and they begin dating. As time passed, the NASA engineers and researchers worked tirelessly on Project Mercury. Goble was the woman in charge of the trajectory of the rocket. It is important to note that Goble was the very first woman from Langley's Aerospace Mechanic Division to be the author of a report. We also read that she and Jim got married in 1959.

The story then jumps to Mary Jackson and her son, Levi, both immersed in making the perfect car for the 1960 soap box derby. Even though that it was a custom that the father helped build the derby car, and it was very unusual for African American boys to enter the race, Jackson did not let either of these obstacles to stop her. She put in the same amount of determination to work to help African American men and women at Langley, and to reach out to African American schoolgirls and girl scouts. Jackson was delighted when she saw that Levi won the soap box derby. She was not happy only because her son had won, but also because Levi was the first African American to win the derby. She knew very well that this win meant that another obstacle for African American equality had been overcome.

PART 10: THE FIRST MAN IN SPACE

The story moves to 1960, where we read about college students in North Carolina who began protesting racial inequality with sit-ins. The sit-ins spread to the entire Hampton Institute, the same place where Christine Mann began participating as well. Mann also helped with voter registration drives. She wanted to encourage as many African Americans as possible to register so they could vote for John F. Kennedy. Langley had also participated and its employees started accepting more men into the computing field. Vaughn was concerned that this may lead to the end of her job, so she started learning how to be a computer programmer.

In 1961, a Soviet cosmonaut became the first person in space and also the first person to orbit the Earth. This encouraged NASA to work even harder on Project Mercury. Alan Shepherd soon became the first American astronaut in space. Several weeks after their first space flight, President Kennedy announced that the US should focus on traveling to the moon. After this NASA moved their headquarters to Huston.

ANALYSIS

Hidden Figures is truly an exceptional and inspiring read in so many ways. First of all, the book deals with several problems that many African American people had to face during the first half of the 20th century. The most prominent problem was definitely racial segregation. Other problems were connected to stereotypes, male vs. female problems, and others, but all of these have their source in racial segregation.

The story begins with a prologue, where we read about the author of the book - Mrs. Margot Lee Shetterly. We read about her visit to Hampton, Virginia, and what exactly influenced her to write a book about hidden figures. And as we read the book – partly biographical and partly autobiographical – we slowly discover the true nature of the book: Hidden Figures is about those who are unseen, those who are perceived as less important, and less human than others.

As we read the book, we are introduced into the lives of several African American women and their roles and influence in the lives of all African Americans and the world. The most influential character is definitely Dorothy Vaughn. Vaughn had a difficult past, just like many other African Americans of that time, but she managed to persevere. Even though she had to face the challenge of abandoning everything she knew and going into the unknown, she knew what her choice will be and why. As we see through the book, if it were not for Vaughn, who knows how NACA's segregation problem and the overall travel to space and moon would look like, and how much time it would take for American to travel to outer space?

Besides Dorothy, there were other women who also greatly contributed to the fact that NASA eventually succeeded in sending a man to space and launching a rocket to the moon.

Katherine Goble (later Johnson) and Mary Jackson were two other very important characters.

There are several very noticeable themes in this book. One of such theme is determination. We can see that theme when we read about the African American women and their contributions. The women not only helped their country to win the space race against the Soviet Union, but also did their best to help end racial segregation in their generation and for future generations. The second theme is patriotism. Jackson, Vaughn, Goble and the others wanted their country to win the war and the space race. But they also needed to face many challenges, because it is difficult to love a country if that country does not love you back.

Overall, Hidden Figures is educational and a very powerful book filled with themes and messages. Even if readers do not love biographies, this book could change their minds.

QUIZ

Welcome to our short quiz about Hidden Figures. Every question is based on our summary, which means you can find all answers there. If you have trouble finding them there, you can find them in the quiz answers section below.

QUESTION 1

What was the codename of NASA's plan for traveling to outer space and landing on the moon?

a) Project Manhattan
b) Project Virgo
c) Project Mercury
d) Project Pluto

QUESTION 2

What was the main cause for the Soviets' success in sending their man into outer space before the Americans?

a) The Soviets had more manpower.
b) The Americans had problems with racial segregation.
c) It was a matter of pure luck.
d) The Soviets sent a spy and managed to get a copy of American space travelling plans.

QUESTION 3

Why was Mary Jackson so eager for her son, Levi, to win the race?

a) Because she knew that if he won, they would get the money, and they needed the money.
b) Jackson knew that winning the race would also mean that her son will be more respected, as well as African Americans in general.
c) a and b.
d) Mary wanted to get even for last year's defeat, when Levi was so close to win.

QUESTION 4

What was the name of a town that Dorothy Vaughn arrived in before she started working at Langley?

a) Newport
b) Huston
c) Scranton
d) Newport News

QUESTION 5

"Dorothy found herself immersed in her studies about aerodynamics and wind tunnels."

TRUE FALSE

QUESTION 6

Why did NACA change their name to NASA?

a) NACA's primary purpose was the research of supersonic speeds and wind tunnels, while NASA's primary goal was the speed of sound.
b) NASA was the successor to NACA. The name was changed after it was decided that the institute would now focus only on space travel.
c) a and b.
d) None of the above.

QUESTION 7

"Thanks to her persistence and intelligence, Katherine Goble was given a permanent position at the Flight Research Division."

TRUE FALSE

QUIZ ANSWERS

QUESTION 1 – c

QUESTION 2 – b

QUESTION 3 – b

QUESTION 4 – d

QUESTION 5 – TRUE

QUESTION 6 – b

QUESTION 7 – TRUE

CONCLUSION

Hidden Figures is a partial biography and partial autobiography written by Margot Lee Shetterly, about several women who greatly contributed to America sending a man to space and the moon. The book is a combination of the life stories of several African American women who worked as hidden figures, but who were more than that: they were heroes.

Written in reader-friendly manner, the book is a message to many and holds strong value, not just for African American people, but for everyone.

Thank You, and more...

Thank you for spending the time to read this book. I hope you hold a greater knowledge of ***Hidden Figures.***

There are many individuals just like you who would like to learn about ***Hidden Figures,*** this information can be useful for them as well so I would highly appreciate it if you post a good review on Amazon Kindle where you purchased this book and share it on social media (Facebook, Instagram, etc.)

Not only does it help me make a living, but it helps others obtain this knowledge as well. I would highly appreciate it!

www.amazon.com

We have other summary books available for you as well.

1- Summary – The Gentleman in Moscow
https://www.amazon.com/dp/B071QXT91T

2- Summary – Wheat Belly by The Summary Guy
https://www.amazon.com/dp/B00RIE1Z5K/

3- Summary – How to Stop Worrying & Start Living
https://www.amazon.com/dp/B06VVKCLQ4

4- Summary – The Giver
https://www.amazon.com/dp/B06XZPPN7V/

5- Summary - The Hard Things About Hard Things
https://www.amazon.com/dp/B06Y2WHLKM/

Thank you for taking the time to read this book, please give us a good review on Amazon to support us, so we (my team and I) can make more summaries for you!

https://www.amazon.com/s/ref=nb_sb_noss?url=search-alias=aps&field-keywords=the+summary+guy&rh=i%3Aaps,k%3Athe+summary+guy

---

Feel free to follow us on social media to get notified of future summaries.

1- *Facebook: BookSummaries*

https://www.facebook.com/BookSummaries-1060732983986564/

Or just search BookSummaries on Facebook

2- *Instagram: BookSummaries*

https://www.instagram.com/booksummaries/